20 Answers

∽

The Eucharist

Trent Horn

Catholic
Answers
Press

20 Answers: The Eucharist
Trent Horn
© 2015 Catholic Answers

Unless otherwise noted, Scripture quotations are from the Revised
Standard Version of the Bible, copyright © 1946, 1952, and 1971
National Council of the Churches of Christ in the United States of
America. Used by permission. All rights reserved worldwide.

Published by Catholic Answers, Inc.
2020 Gillespie Way
El Cajon, California 92020
1-888-291-8000 orders
619-387-0042 fax
catholic.com

Printed in the United States of America

978-1-941663-43-1
978-1-941663-44-8 Kindle
978-1-941663-45-5 ePub

Nihil Obstat: Hugh Barbour, O. Praem.
Censor Librorum

Imprimatur: + The Most Reverend Kevin W. Vann J.C.D., D.D.
Bishop, Diocese of Orange

Questions

Introduction

According to the *Catechism of the Catholic Church* (CCC), the Eucharist is uniquely important for Christians; it is "the source and summit of the Christian life" (1324). Even some of the Church's harshest critics also understand the centrality of this doctrine. Former priest Bart Brewer writes, "Of all the ancient dogmas of the Roman Catholic religion, the dogma of transubstantiation is the most wicked and satanic. It is the very heart of Romanism and the key to the so-called 'sacrifice of the mass.'"[1] Atheists find the doctrine of the Eucharist to be especially revolting. In a debate about God and morality, atheist author Sam Harris said:

> This to me is the true horror of religion. It allows perfectly decent and sane people to believe by the billions, what only lunatics could believe on their own. If you wake up tomorrow morning thinking that saying a few Latin words over your pancakes is gonna turn them into the body of Elvis Presley, ok, you have lost your mind. But if you think more or less the same thing about a cracker and the body of Jesus, you're just a Catholic.[2]

It's not just outspoken atheists or critics of the Church who deny the Real Presence of Christ in the

Eucharist. According to one poll, although 91 percent of people who attend Mass weekly say they believe Christ is really present in the Eucharist, only 65 percent of those who attend Mass monthly believe the same thing. In fact, of those who attend Mass a few times during the year, fewer than half believe Christ is truly present in the Eucharist.[3]

Of course, this should be expected, because if a person does not think Christ is truly present in the Eucharist then he will be less motivated to make time each week to receive him in it. Thus the goal of this booklet is to help Catholics and non-Catholics better understand the Eucharist so they can draw closer to Christ through this sacrament.

1. What does the Catholic Church teach about the Eucharist?

The word "Eucharist" comes from the Greek word *eucharistein*, which means "thanksgiving." It is the memorial sacrifice of Christ's body and blood, presented under the form of bread and wine, which is offered to the Father for the forgiveness of sins. After this offering, the Eucharist is consumed, and through this act it transmits sanctifying grace to those who are properly prepared to receive the body and blood of Christ (see Answer 12).

Like baptism or confession, the Eucharist is a sacrament—an outward expression of an inward reception of grace. The *Catechism* teaches that "The Eucharist is the efficacious sign and sublime cause of that communion in the divine life and that unity of the People of God by which the Church is kept in being" (CCC 1325). However, the Eucharist differs from the other sacraments in an important way because it "is 'the source and summit of the Christian life.' The other sacraments, and indeed all ecclesiastical ministries and works of the apostolate, are bound up with the Eucharist and are oriented toward it" (CCC 1324).

For example, the sacrament of baptism and initiates us into the Church so that we may receive the Eucharist. The sacrament of reconciliation spiritually heals us so we can receive the Eucharist after receiving absolution for our sins. The anointing of the sick physically and spiritually heals us so we can receive the Eucharist anew, and sometimes it is accompanied by the last Eucharist we will receive before we depart this life (what is called *viaticum*, which means "on a journey"). Lastly, the sacrament of marriage gives spouses the grace to raise families that partake of the Eucharist, and the sacrament of holy orders gives us the priests who offer up the Eucharist at Mass.

The *Catechism* goes on to say, "For in the blessed Eucharist is contained the whole spiritual good of the Church, namely Christ himself, our Pasch" (CCC 1324). The word *pasch* refers to the Jewish celebration of Passover, and it is no coincidence that the Eucharist commemorates the Passover meal Christ held with his disciples before his Crucifixion. But unlike the old Passover, the Eucharist is our new Passover and represents the sacrifice of the "Lamb of God, who takes away the sins of the world" (John 1:29). And just as the lamb of the old Passover was consumed, Christ, the new Passover lamb, must also be consumed. This is why the Eucharist is also called the "Lord's Supper" or the "Breaking of Bread." As the *Catechism* explains:

[It is called] the *Lord's Supper*, because of its connection with the supper which the Lord took with his disciples on the eve of his Passion and because it anticipates the wedding feast of the Lamb in the heavenly Jerusalem. [It is called] the *Breaking of Bread*, because Jesus used this rite, part of a Jewish meal when as master of the table he blessed and distributed the bread, above all at the Last Supper. It is by this action that his disciples will recognize him after his Resurrection, and it is this expression that the first Christians will use to designate their Eucharistic assemblies; by doing so they signified that all who eat the one broken bread, Christ, enter into communion with him and form but one body in him (CCC 1329).

Finally, this new Passover sacrifice is offered in the context of the Mass. It is called "Mass" because, "the liturgy in which the mystery of salvation is accomplished concludes with the sending forth (*missio*) of the faithful, so that they may fulfill God's will in their daily lives" (CCC 1332). Within that context the Eucharist is also called "the Holy Sacrifice, because it makes present the one sacrifice of Christ the Savior and includes the Church's offering. The terms *holy sacrifice of the Mass, sacrifice of praise, spiritual sacrifice,* and *pure and holy sacrifice* are also used to describe the Eucharist, since it completes and surpasses all the sacrifices of the Old Covenant" (CCC 1330).

2. How do non-Catholic views of the Eucharist differ from the Catholic belief?

Nearly all Christians celebrate some form of the Eucharist by consuming bread and wine in memory of Christ's death and Resurrection. Protestants usually refer to the Eucharist as the Lord's Supper and do not believe that Christ is physically present in the bread and wine at their services or at the Catholic Mass. The various Protestant views on this sacrament can be found along this continuum:

Rejection of the sacrament: Some denominations do not celebrate the Eucharist. For example, the Salvation Army is usually known for its charity work, but it is actually a self-proclaimed Christian denomination.[4] According to an article in the *Los Angeles Times*, "Catherine Booth, the influential wife of the founder [of the Salvation Army], admired the piety and practices of Quakers, who did not perform baptisms or Communion rites. In keeping with the Salvation Army's theology of sanctification—the Holy Spirit active in the lives of holy people— she saw all of life as sacramental. Although he did not prohibit the sacraments, William Booth declared in 1883 that the rites would not be endorsed as official worship of the Army."[5]

A memorial dinner: This view is common among Baptists and other "born-again" Christians. According to one Baptist writer, "the Supper functions as proclamation, the presence of Christ in the indwelling Spirit not only assures forgiveness through the Word; he also convicts of unbiblical patterns of life and thought."[6] According to this view, the Eucharist is a sign that points us to Christ, but Christ is not present in the Eucharist. Instead, Christ is present in the "indwelling Spirit" of the believer who receives the Eucharist.

A real, nonphysical presence: The Reformed tradition observed by Presbyterians holds that Christ is actually present in the Eucharist, but not in a physical way. In 1647, the Westminster Confession of Faith, a popular confession made by those in the Reformed tradition, said that "Worthy receivers, outwardly partaking of the visible elements, in this sacrament, do then also, inwardly by faith, really and indeed, *yet not carnally and corporally, but spiritually* [emphasis added], receive and feed upon Christ crucified, and all benefits of his death."[7] This can be considered a "conduit view," since Christ's body isn't *located* in the bread and wine but is instead made *manifest* through them.

A sacramental union: In contrast to the Reformed position, Martin Luther held a stronger position on the Real Presence of Christ in the Eucharist. He claimed that the bread and wine exist in the Eucharist in a natural state while the body and blood of Christ exist in those same objects in a supernatural state. According to Luther, "Why then should we not much more say in the Supper, 'This is my body,' even though bread and body are two distinct substances, and the word 'this' indicates the bread? Here, too, out of two kinds of objects a union has taken place, which I shall call a 'sacramental union,' because Christ's body and the bread are given to us as a sacrament."[8] In other words, the consecrated bread and wine fully *contain* Christ's body and blood, but they do not become Christ's body and blood.

A physical change: The Catholic view of the Eucharist is different from the Protestant views because Catholics believe that the bread and wine at Mass actually become the physical body and blood of Christ. After consecration, the bread and wine no longer remain, and in their place is the body, blood, soul, and divinity of Jesus Christ. The Council of Trent taught that in the Eucharist there is a change "of the whole substance of the bread into the substance of the body of Christ our Lord, and of the whole substance of the wine into the substance of his blood."[9]

Eastern Orthodox churches hold the same view of the Eucharist as Catholics, but they sometimes use different vocabulary when describing the physical change from bread and wine into body and blood.[10] Because Eastern Orthodox priests retain valid holy orders despite not being in union with the pope, and because they also subscribe to a belief in Christ's Real Presence in the Eucharist, a Catholic in an emergency situation (e.g., in danger of death) may receive the Eucharist at an Orthodox service (see Answer 14).

3. Why do Catholics believe the Eucharist is the physical body and blood of Christ when it looks exactly like bread and wine?

In order to understand why Catholics believe the Eucharist becomes the actual body and blood of Christ after it is consecrated at Mass, we must understand two philosophical ideas; *substance* and *accident*. A substance is what something is: an accident is what a substance possesses. So, for example, an apple (a substance) has many accidents. It has a skin of a particular color, a certain weight, shape, taste, and so on. These accidents are what we perceive with our senses, but an apple is more than just a bundle of accidents. These accidents could change, and the apple would remain an apple (that is, the apple could come in a different color or size). These ever-changing accidents are united within one unchanging substance that ceases to exist only when the apple ceases to exist (such as when it is eaten and digested).

When it comes to the Eucharist, the Church teaches that after consecration the substance of the bread and wine—what these objects are at their metaphysical core—changes and becomes the body and blood of Christ. But although the substance of the bread and wine changes, the accidents of the bread and wine— what we perceive of these substances—remain. This is why the eucharistic host still looks and tastes like bread and the precious blood still looks and tastes like wine. The bread and wine have not *transformed*, because the form or appearance of the bread and wine has not changed. Instead, it is the substance of the bread and wine that has changed, and so Catholics teach that during consecration the bread and wine have been *transubstantiated* into the body and blood of Christ.

However, the sixteenth-century Protestant Reformers rejected transubstantiation, believing that it was unbiblical and nonsensical. Luther said, "[I]t is an absurd and unheard-of juggling with words, to understand 'bread' to mean 'the form, or accidents of bread,' and 'wine' to mean 'the form, or accidents of wine.'

Why do they not also understand all other things to mean their forms, or accidents?"[11]

The answer to Luther's question is that Jesus referred to the bread as his body and the wine as his blood. Jesus did not say, "This bread *contains* my body" or "I am *in* this wine." Jesus just said the bread and wine *were* his body and blood. But because we still perceive the bread and wine at Mass to be bread and wine, and because Jesus says this is not bread and wine but his flesh and blood, then the only logical conclusion is that although the accidents of the bread and wine that we perceive have remained, the substance, or what these things are, has changed into Christ's body and blood.

Other critics of this doctrine object that the term *transubstantiation* is found neither in the Bible nor in the writings of the Church Fathers for the first thousand years of the Church's history. But the reason the term was not used among the early Church Fathers was that there was no disagreement among them about the nature of the Eucharist. They unanimously agreed that the Eucharist represented in a physical and real way the body and blood of Christ (see Answer 8).

Moreover, it was common in Church history for doctrines to be officially defined (and terms to be created for those definitions) only when heresy had to be combated. For example, the doctrines of the Trinity and the Incarnation of Christ were not defined until centuries after the time of the apostles because they were not seriously challenged until then. In order to respond to these trinitarian and Christological disputes, Catholic theologians developed extrabiblical language to help them explain doctrine and refute heretics. Terms such as *homoousios*, which describes the one divine substance that belongs equally to each person of the Trinity, and *hypostatic union*, which describes the complete union of Christ's divine and human natures, are examples of this.

Something similar happened with the Eucharist. In the eleventh century, a monk named Berengar of Tours argued that the bread and wine became only symbols of the body and blood of Christ. In response to teachings like his, the Church declared at the Fourth Lateran Council (1215) that "his body and blood are truly contained in the sacrament of the altar under the forms of bread and wine, the bread and wine having been *transubstantiated*, by God's power, into his body and blood."[12]

This teaching was later defined at the Council of Trent in 1551, which taught that "by the consecration of the bread and of the wine, a conversion is made of the whole substance of the bread into the substance of the body of Christ our Lord, and of the whole substance of the wine into the substance of his blood; which conversion is, by the holy Catholic Church, suitably and properly called Transubstantiation."[13]

4. If the Eucharist contains the physical presence of Christ's body and blood, doesn't that mean Catholics who eat it are cannibals?

This is actually a very old charge against Christians that dates all the way back to pagan critics of the early Church. In the third century, Origen accused the pagan critic Celsus of acting "like those Jews who, when Christianity began to be first preached, scattered abroad false reports of the Gospel, such as that Christians offered up an infant in sacrifice, and partook of its flesh."[14] In the second century, Justin Martyr responded to Jewish critics who accused Christians of "fabulous and shameful deeds—the upsetting of the lamp, and promiscuous intercourse, and eating human flesh."[15]

Regardless of how the charge of cannibalism arose, it was as false then as it is now. That's because consuming the body and blood Christ under the form of bread and wine does not fall under the definition of cannibalism. *Merriam-Webster* defines cannibalism as "the usually ritualistic eating of human flesh by a human being,"[16] but there are several important differences that prove Catholic are not cannibals. First, cannibals eat the substance of ordinary human flesh under the form of flesh. Catholics consume the glorified human flesh of Christ under the form of bread and wine. Second, the victim of cannibalism is often killed; then only the parts that provide temporal nourishment are consumed. The soul is not consumed (since it is immaterial and departs from the body at death) and the inedible body parts are discarded. But those who consume the Eucharist do not kill Christ, and Christ's person is not consumed in part like a victim of cannibalism. Instead, the communicant receives Christ's whole person—his body, blood, soul, and divinity, and, unlike the temporal nourishment provided to the body through cannibalism, the Eucharist provides the communicant with spiritual nourishment that leads to eternal life.

Another important point to remember is that a symbolic interpretation of the Eucharist does not escape this objection either. Even if Jesus were not physically present in the Eucharist, the fact that the Eucharist symbolically represents his body and blood would mean that Protestants were taking part in *symbolic* cannibalism. But Christ would never command his followers to symbolically act out an evil like cannibalism any more than he would instruct his followers to symbolically act out an evil like rape or murder. The simple truth is that Christ did not command us to be cannibals, either literally or symbolically. He instead commanded us to receive him in a bodily way as the new Passover lamb.

Finally, because Christ is the God-man, we don't relate to him as we would a fellow human. Worshipping a man, for example, would normally be idolatry, but if that man is God, as is the case with Jesus Christ, then it's not idolatry. Likewise, eating a man would normally be cannibalism, but if that man is God and he has given us his body in a miraculous way for our spiritual benefit, then consuming him is not cannibalism. In fact, it would be a sin to *disobey* God's direct command to eat his body and blood so that we may have life through him.

5. Wasn't Jesus commanding the apostles to host a perpetual memorial dinner in his honor instead of commanding them to literally eat his body and blood?

When this question is asked it betrays either-or thinking. Specifically, it forces us to accept the false dilemma that *either* the Eucharist is a memorial dinner in honor of Christ *or* that it is a sacrifice involving his literal body and blood. But why can't it be both? The Church teaches that the Eucharist is certainly a memorial meal, but it is not *only* a memorial.

According to the *Catechism*:

At the Last Supper, on the night he was betrayed, our Savior instituted the Eucharistic sacrifice of his Body and Blood. This he did in order to perpetuate the sacrifice of the cross throughout the ages until he should come again, and so to entrust to his beloved

Spouse, the Church, a memorial of his death and Resurrection: a sacrament of love, a sign of unity, a bond of charity, a Paschal banquet in which Christ is consumed, the mind is filled with grace, and a pledge of future glory is given to us (CCC 1323).

Jesus said, "Do this in memory of me," and the words "in memory" come from the Greek word *anamnesis*, which means more than a mental recollection of a past event or person. It means, instead, a "remembrance brought about by the act of sacrifice."[17] An example of this can be found in Leviticus 24:7-8, in which the Israelite priest and his sons are instructed to offer a memorial sacrifice of bread to the Lord each Sabbath. The verses say, "[Y]ou shall put pure frankincense with each row, that it may go with the bread as a memorial [*anamnesis*] portion to be offered by fire to the Lord. Every sabbath day Aaron shall set it in order before the Lord continually on behalf of the sons of Israel as a covenant forever." The original Hebrew word for memorial in this passage, *azkarah*, also means "memorial offering."

The parallel between this and the sacrifice of the Mass, at which holy bread is offered on the new Sabbath to commemorate the new, everlasting covenant in Christ, is uncanny. Similarly when Jesus said, "Do this in memory of me," he did not mean simply, "Remember me when you eat this meal." A more accurate translation of Jesus' command would be, "Receive me as a memorial sacrifice." The first Christians, who were raised in Judaism, would have had no difficulty understanding that a memorial dinner can bring about the actual presence of God. Bible scholar Brant Pitre puts it this way:

> Just as God had been really present to his people in the tabernacle of Moses and the temple of Solomon, so now Jesus would be really and truly present to his disciples through the Eucharist. And just as the old bread of the Presence had been the sign of God's "everlasting covenant," so now the Eucharist would become the perpetual sign of the new covenant, sealed in his blood.[18]

One final objection to the idea that Christ was instituting a sacrifice and not just a memorial meal was that Jesus was present at the Last Supper. How could Jesus have offered up a sacrifice of himself when the apostles could still see him? Did Jesus receive himself at the Last Supper?

The synoptic Gospels describe Jesus and the apostles eating this meal as a group, so it is improbable that Jesus abstained while the others ate. But how could Christ receive his own body and blood? It's important to remember that Christ's physical presence in the Eucharist is not limited by space and time. Dominican theologian Giles Dimock says, "[Christ] is not present in a merely physical way, but more like that of a glorified body, which according to St. Thomas, has qualities beyond the physical, without forsaking its bodiliness."[19]

This ability to transcend the spatial and the temporal allowed Christ to be physically present both in a human body before the disciples and also in the bread at the Last Supper. St. Thomas Aquinas said it was fitting that Christ would receive himself at the Last Supper, "Because Christ himself was the first to fulfill what he required others to observe: hence he willed first to be baptized when imposing baptism upon others: as we read in Acts 1:1: 'Jesus began to do and to teach.' Hence he first of all took his own body and blood, and afterwards gave it to be taken by the disciples."[20]

Finally, the New Testament gives us abundant evidence that Jesus envisioned the bread that would be offered in the Eucharist as something other than ordinary bread. For example, several Church Fathers translated the phrase "Give us this day our daily bread" (Matt. 6:11) as "Give us this day our *supernatural* bread," to more closely align with the original Greek text.[21] Moreover, when Jesus appeared to the disciples on the road to Emmaus, he hid his identity until after he blessed and broke bread with them. In other words, Jesus made it clear that after his Resurrection his disciples would not see Jesus in a human form, but that he would instead be "known to them in the breaking of the bread" (Luke 24:35).

6. Is the Bread of Life discourse in John 6 evidence for the Real Presence?

Unlike the Gospels of Matthew, Mark, and Luke, John's Gospel does not contain a description of the Last Supper. Instead, John offered a teaching of Jesus that complements what the other Gospels tell us in their depictions of the Last Supper.

John 6 takes place after Jesus miraculously fed 5,000 people. The bread of life passage begins with a group of people following him because of this miracle. Christ knows that they seek more bread, so he tells them, "I am the bread of life; he who comes to me shall not hunger, and he who believes in me shall never thirst" (John 6:35). They still question Jesus about who he is, which prompts him to answer, "I am the living bread which came down from heaven; if any one eats of this bread, he will live forever; and the bread which I shall give for the life of the world is my flesh" (John 6:51).

We could take Jesus to mean that his "bread" is the body he will offer up on the cross for the sins of the world. But then Jesus makes his real point abundantly clear when the people ask, "How can this man give us his flesh to eat?" Jesus tells them:

Truly, truly, I say to you, unless you eat the flesh of the Son of man and drink his blood, you have no life in you; he who eats my flesh and drinks my blood has eternal life, and I will raise him up at the last day. For my flesh is food indeed, and my blood is drink indeed. He who eats my flesh and drinks my blood abides in me, and I in him. As the living Father sent me, and I live because of the Father, so he who eats me will live because of me (John 6:53-57).

The original Greek here communicates an even more powerful message than what we read in English. Earlier in the passage Jesus uses *phago*, a generic word for eating, but in these verses he switches to *trogo*, which means "to gnaw or chew." Likewise, Jesus uses the word *sarx*, which means the soft, fleshy substance that covers the body, and not *soma,* which just means "body." His word choice, as rendered in the Greek, underscores that he is talking about real, physical chewing and eating.

In response to this interpretation of the passage, some people say that Jesus was speaking symbolically. Because in verse 35 Jesus said, "He who comes to me will never hunger and he who believes in me will never thirst," these critics infer that by "eating" Jesus means to "come to him spiritually" and that by "drinking his blood" he means "believing in Jesus by faith."[22] But the Bread of Life discourse is not only one section with one meaning. Verses 1 to 47 are indeed symbolic in nature, with Jesus using earthly metaphors to teach the importance of believing in him.

But it doesn't make sense to say that Jesus was being symbolic throughout the discourse. In verse 35, for example, Jesus said that whoever believes in him will never thirst, which makes us think of water. Jesus could have continued to refer to himself as a source of living water that we should drink, as he does in John 4:14 and John 7:37-38. Instead, Jesus tells us to drink his *blood,* an act that had been forbidden since the days of Noah (Gen. 9:4). Furthermore, the Hebrew idiom "to eat one's flesh" means to curse or revile someone (cf. Micah 3:3). If Jesus were being symbolic and not literal, then his words "eat my flesh" would mean he wanted us to curse him and break God's law in order to gain eternal life.

A more plausible explanation than the symbolic one is that Jesus was literally referring to manna, or heavenly food, throughout the entire discourse. As Brant Pitre argues in his book *Jesus and the Jewish Roots of the Eucharist,* many ancient Jews expected a Davidic messiah who would overthrow Israel's oppressors, but other Jews expected a Mosaic messiah who would inaugurate a new Exodus and lead Israel to a new heavenly promised land. One of the signs of the Mosaic messiah would be his ability to produce manna, the miraculous bread that fell from heaven and fed the Israelites in the wilderness after they left Egypt (Exod. 16).

In John 6:49, Jesus spoke of providing the people with bread that is superior to the old manna. As Pitre says:

If the old manna was the miraculous "food of the angels," could the new manna be just ordinary bread and wine? If so, that would make the old manna *greater* than the new! . . . If Jesus had wanted his Jewish disciples to regard the Eucharist as ordinary food and drink, he would certainly never have identified it as the new manna from heaven.[23]

Finally, John told us that, "After this many of his disciples drew back and no longer went about with him" (John 6:66). Even the disciples questioned Jesus' teaching, but Jesus did not reassure them that he was being symbolic. He had done this on another occasion, when the disciples thought Jesus was talking about literal food when he was actually speaking metaphorically about doing the Father's will (John 4:32-34). In the case of the Bread of Life discourse, Jesus reaffirmed the difficulty of this teaching, and the disciples continued to follow him, because they knew he had, as Peter said, "the words of eternal life" (John 6:68–69).

7. What are some common objections to the biblical evidence for the Eucharist?

Perhaps the most common objection to the biblical evidence for the Eucharist is the observation that Jesus routinely used self-referential metaphors that

Catholics don't take literally. For example, Protestant apologists Norman Geisler and Ralph MacKenzie note that Jesus said, "I am the door" (John 10:7) and "I am the vine" (John 15:5), yet, in their words, "Roman Catholic scholars do not take these statements literally, even though they come from the same book that records 'This is my body!' It is therefore, not necessary to take Jesus literally when he said 'this is my body' or 'eat my flesh.'"[24]

The problem with Geisler and MacKenzie's argument is that it can be taken too far. If any of Jesus' commands are too demanding or strange they can simply be written off as metaphors since Christ used metaphors on some occasions. Of course, the question isn't whether Christ spoke metaphorically. The question is did he speak metaphorically *in this instance*?

First, notice that Jesus does not continually refer to himself as a door or a vine in the same way that he continually and emphatically tells his audience that they must eat his flesh. Second, Christ does not tell us to "oil his *true* hinges" or "water his *true* roots" in John 10 and 15. This stands in contrast to his command that we eat his body as "true food" and drink his blood as "true drink." Finally, no one rejected Christ for using metaphors involving the door or the vine, but when he declared that one must eat his flesh in order to have eternal life "many of his disciples drew back and no longer went about with him" (John 6:66). The fact that these followers abandoned Jesus shows that they did not misunderstand him; they took his claims literally and chose to reject them.

Another common objection comes from John 6:63. Geisler and MacKenzie say that this verse resolves the entire interpretation of the Bread of Life passage because here Jesus says, "It is the spirit that gives life, the flesh is of no avail; the words that I have spoken to you are spirit and life." According to critics like them, this means that Jesus did not literally command us to eat his flesh, since the flesh "counts for nothing." Instead, Jesus only wants us to believe the words he spoke, since his words are "spirit and life."[25]

The problem with this objection is that what Jesus meant by "spirit" and "flesh" is different from what we mean by those terms today. For us, spirit and flesh tend to be synonyms for "immaterial" and "material." But the New Testament frequently uses "spirit" to mean not what a thing is composed of (or a ghostly, spiritual substance), but what it is ordered toward, what its ultimate "end" is. The spirit is that which is ordered to the things that are "above" or that are in the spiritual world. The "flesh," on the other hand, refers to that which is corruptible and ordered to the material world. Paul talks about spiritual people who judge all things but are judged by no one (1 Cor. 2:15) as well as men of the flesh (1 Cor. 3:1), but both these groups are composed of people with physical bodies.

Catholic apologist Karl Keating summarizes the futility involved in using John 6:63 to invalidate the Catholic understanding of the Eucharist. He writes:

[Did fundamentalists] think that Christ, who had just commanded his disciples to eat his flesh, now said their doing so would be pointless? Is that what "the flesh is of no avail" means? "Eat my flesh, but you'll find it's a waste of time"—is that how he was to be understood? And were the disciples to understand the line "the words I have been speaking to you are spirit, and life" as nothing but a circumlocution, and a fairly clumsy one at that, for 'symbolic'?[26]

Finally, notice that Jesus never said "my flesh" counts for nothing. He only says that *the flesh*—the corrupted material aspects of this world—counts for nothing. Rejecting the Eucharist because it looks like bread and wine—that is, making a material rather than a spiritual judgment—is what counts for nothing. Instead, Jesus' words "eat my flesh and drink my blood" are spirit and life, and by heeding them we have eternal life.

8. What did the early Church Fathers believe about the Eucharist?

Acts 2:42 tells us that the early Christians "devoted themselves to the apostles' teaching and fellowship, to the breaking of bread and the prayers." According to Protestant church historian J.N.D. Kelly, early Christians' teaching on the Eucharist "was in general unquestioningly realist, i.e., the consecrated bread and wine were taken to be, and were treated and designated as, the Saviour's body and blood."[27] Anglican scholar Darwell Stone also makes the same point and says, "Throughout the writings of the Fathers there is unbroken agreement that the consecrated bread and wine are the body and blood of Christ, and that the Eucharist is a sacrifice."[28]

Here are just a few excerpts from the early Church Fathers that demonstrate their agreement on this issue:

- *St. Ignatius of Antioch, A.D. 110*—"[Heretics] abstain from the Eucharist and from prayer because they do not confess that the Eucharist is the flesh of our Savior Jesus Christ, flesh which suffered for our sins and which the Father, in his goodness, raised up again. They who deny the gift of God are perishing in their disputes."[29]

- *St. Justin Martyr, A.D. 151*—"As we have been taught, the food which has been made into the Eucharist by the eucharistic prayer set down by him, and by the change of which our blood and flesh is nurtured, is both the flesh and the blood of that incarnated Jesus."[30]

- *St. Irenaeus, A.D. 189*—"If the Lord were from other than the Father, how could he rightly take bread, which is of the same creation as our own, and confess it to be his body and affirm that the mixture in the cup is his blood?"[31]

- *Origen, A.D. 248*—"Formerly, in an obscure way, there was manna for food; now, however, in full view, there is the true food, the flesh of the Word of God, as he himself says: 'My flesh is true food, and my blood is true drink' [John 6:55]."[32]

Despite the overwhelming evidence that there was unanimous belief among the Church Fathers that Christ is physically present in the Eucharist, some writers distort the historical record to suit their own agendas. Consider, for example, the writings of Bart Brewer. In his tract *The Mystery of the Eucharist* he claims, "The idea of a corporal presence [in the Eucharist] was vaguely held by some, such as Ambrose."[33] But consider the following excerpt from Ambrose and ask yourself if Christ's physical presence is only "vaguely held" in it:

Why do you seek the order of nature in the Body of Christ, seeing that the Lord Jesus himself was born of a Virgin, not according to nature? *It is the true Flesh of Christ which was crucified and buried, this is then truly the Sacrament of his Body* [emphasis added].[34]

Other critics take out of context what the Fathers wrote in order to imply that some of them believed only in a symbolic presence of Christ in the Eucharist. For example, Protestant apologist William Webster says that the third-century Church Father Tertullian "spoke of the bread and wine in the Eucharist as symbols and figures which represent the body and blood of Christ. He specifically stated that these were not the literal body and blood of the Lord."[35] Webster is appealing to this passage in Tertullian's *Against Marcion*: "Then, having taken the bread and given it to his disciples, he made it his own body, by saying, 'This is my body,' that is, the figure of my body. A figure, however, there could not have been, unless there were first a veritable body."[36]

The problem with Webster's interpretation is that Tertullian is attacking the heretic Marcion, who claimed that Christ was not actually human but had a phantom or unreal body. If this were the case, then the Eucharist could not be a sign of Christ's body because Christ never had a body at all! When Church Fathers, like Tertullian, use words such as "sign" or "figure" they do not mean the Eucharist is only symbolic. As Kelly notes, "It must not be supposed, of course, that this 'symbolical' language implied that the bread and wine were regarded as mere pointers to, or tokens of, absent realities. Rather were they accepted as signs of realities which were somehow actually present though apprehended by faith alone."[37]

Webster himself admits that "As time passed clearer descriptions of the Eucharist as the transformation of the elements into the literal body and blood of Christ emerged in the writings of the Fathers such as Cyril of Jerusalem, Gregory of Nyssa, Gregory Nazianzen, Chrysostom and Ambrose."[38]

9. Was the Eucharist copied from pagan religions?

There are two kinds of critics who claim that the sacrament of the Eucharist was borrowed from pagan religions: anti-Catholic Protestants who believe that distinctly Catholic beliefs come from pagan mythology, and Jesus "mythicists" who believe that Jesus never existed and that anything related to him was borrowed from that same mythology.

Bart Brewer represents a position typical of anti-Catholic Evangelicals when he says that after the conversion of Constantine and the legalization of Christianity, "[new converts] brought with them pagan rites which they boldly introduced into the church with Christian terminology, thus corrupting the primitive faith."[39] But many of the "rites" the Church adopted are harmless customs, such as styles of vestments or temple architecture. (Protestants do the same thing when they exchange wedding rings, because this practice is not found in Scripture but is found in ancient Roman sources.) More to the point, we've already seen that the "pure and faithful" pre-Constantine Church Brewer speaks of did believe in the Real Presence of the Eucharist (along with many other distinctly Catholic doctrines).

The anti-Catholic author Jack Chick makes even more astounding assertions than Brewer in his tract about the Eucharist called *The Death Cookie*. Chick says the Eucharist was taken from the Egyptian practice of worshipping the sun god Osiris in the form of "round sun-shaped wafers made of unleavened bread." He even claims that the monogram IHS imprinted on the host stands for "Isis, Horus, and Seb, the gods of Egypt."[40] But Chick doesn't footnote or document any of these claims, and for good reason—they are completely without merit.

First, Osiris was not the sun god (that title belonged to Ra), and so there were no "sun-shaped" wafers made in his honor, and reputable Egyptologists know nothing of Osiris being transubstantiated into a Eucharist. Second, the monogram has nothing to do with Egyptian mythology. *I*, *H*, and *S* are the first three letters in the Greek version of Jesus' name.[41] Finally, wafers and cakes offered in the Old Testament were presumably also round, but no Protestant would say they were pagan in origin (Gen. 18:1–8; Exod. 29:1–2).

The Jesus mythicists frequently quote the following passage from St. Justin Martyr: "He said, 'This is my blood'; and gave it to them alone. Which the wicked devils have imitated in the mysteries of Mithras, commanding the same thing to be done. For, that bread and a cup of water are placed with certain incantations in the mystic rites of one who is being initiated, you either know or can learn."[42]

According to the mythicists, Mithraists celebrated the Eucharist long before Christians did and so Justin is ignorant of the fact that it was actually *Christians* who copied this sacrament from paganism, and not pagans devilishly copying Christians. However, Mithraic scholar Manfred Clauss tells us that "there can be no question of imitation in either direction. The offering of bread and wine is known in virtually all ancient cultures, and the meal as a means of binding the faithful together and uniting them to the deity was a feature common to many religions. . . . The ritual meal was probably simply a component of regular common meals. Such meals have always been an essential part of religious assembly."[43]

St. Paul tells us that Christians took part in a communal meal before receiving the Eucharist (this was often called an agape feast or a "love feast"). Paul chastised the Corinthians for using such occasions to become drunk and gluttonous while others went hungry. Of course, Christians did not "borrow" the concept of a communal meal from pagans, since all people have a natural desire to share food in a communal setting. The Mithraic "communion meal" was simply that, a communal meal. Clauss writes, "Mithraists did not just receive bread and wine or water, as the literary sources seem to suggest, but were in addition served actual meals."[44]

More to the point, if there were any borrowing, it would be from Christianity to Mithraism, since the Roman Mithra cult came after Jesus and had no connection to the Persian Mithra cult that existed before the time of Christ.[45]

Ironically, when fundamentalist Protestants and atheists make the "pagan-influence" argument they both make the same mistake. They strain to locate similarities between the Church and paganism and argue that it is always the Catholic Faith that came from paganism. They don't admit that borrowing took place in the opposite direction, or that the similarities are superficial and so no borrowing took place at all.

10. Why do Catholics sacrifice Christ in the form of the Eucharist when Scripture plainly teaches that Christ has been sacrificed "once and for all"?

There is no contradiction in the Mass's being called a holy sacrifice and Scripture's testimony that Christ was offered as a sacrifice *once* on Calvary to atone for sins. The resolution of this apparent contradiction is found in the fact that Christ is not sacrificed anew at every Mass, but *re-presented* to the Father for the atonement of sin. According to Pope St. John Paul II, "The Eucharist is indelibly marked by the event of the Lord's Passion and death, of which it is not only a reminder but the sacramental re-presentation. It is the sacrifice of the Cross perpetuated down the ages."[46]

The letter to the Hebrews is clear that, unlike the animal sacrifices of the Old Testament, Christ's sacrifice was perfect and does not need to be repeated on a continual basis. In other words, Christ does not have to be crucified again and again in order to atone for our sins. Hebrews 9:27–28 says that "just as it is appointed for men to die once, and after that comes judgment, so Christ, having been offered once to bear the sins of many."

Romans 8:34 says, "Christ Jesus who died—more than that, who was raised to life—is at the right hand of God and is *also interceding for us* [emphasis added]." But if Christ's one sacrifice was accomplished at the Crucifixion and was completely sufficient to take away sin, then why would Christ be interceding for Christians thirty years after his Crucifixion, when Paul wrote his letter to the Romans?

The answer lies in the distinction between "bloody" and "unbloody" sacrifice. Christ offered only one "bloody" sacrifice, when he, the sacrificial victim, was painfully slain. This one perfect sacrifice is continually re-presented to the Father in an unbloody way through the miracle of the Eucharist. Hebrews 13:10

even reveals that Christians "have an altar from which those who serve the tent have no right to eat." If Christ were only "sacrificed once," then Christians would not have any sacrificial altars since there would be no need for other sacrifices. Instead, this means that Jewish priests who serve in the temple may not partake in the unbloody eucharistic sacrifice that is offered on Christian altars.

The early Church Fathers taught that the Eucharist was a sacrifice offered by priests for the forgiveness of sins. The first-century author of the *Didache* advised Christians to "break bread and offer the Eucharist; but first make confession of your faults, so that your sacrifice may be a pure one."[47] The Church Fathers understood that Christ's role as our high priest (Heb. 4:14–16) did not take away from the new ministerial priesthood in Christ. In the third century, St. Cyprian of Carthage said, "If Christ Jesus, our Lord and God, is himself the high priest of God the Father; and if he offered himself as a sacrifice to the Father; and if he commanded that this be done in commemoration of himself, then certainly the priest, who imitates that which Christ did, truly functions in place of Christ."[48]

St. Augustine gives us a clear example of how our belief in Christ's unique sacrifice on the cross can be represented in the liturgy of the Mass. He said, "Was not Christ once for all offered up in his own person as a sacrifice? And yet, is he not likewise offered up in the sacrament as a sacrifice, not only in the special solemnities of Easter, but also daily among our congregations; so that the man who, being questioned, answers that he is offered as a sacrifice in that ordinance, declares what is strictly true? For if sacraments had not some points of real resemblance to the things of which they are the sacraments, they would not be sacraments at all."[49]

11. What happens when the Eucharist is consecrated at Mass?

According to the U.S. Conference of Catholic Bishops, "The Eucharistic Prayer is the heart of the Liturgy of the Eucharist. In this prayer, the celebrant acts in the person of Christ as head of his body, the Church. He gathers not only the bread and the wine, but the substance of our lives and joins them to Christ's perfect sacrifice, offering them to the Father."[50]

The *General Instruction of the Roman Missal* (GIRM) lists the following elements in the Eucharistic Prayer:

• The *thanksgiving:* The priest, in the name of all God's people, glorifies and gives thanks to the Father. The priest then gives thanks for the whole work of salvation or for some particular aspect of it, according to the liturgical season in which the Mass is being celebrated.

- The *acclamation:* The congregation joins with the choir of angels and saints in heaven and recites the *Sanctus* (Holy, Holy, Holy).

- The *epiclesis:* The Church implores the power of the Holy Spirit to cause the gifts offered by human hands to become Christ's Body and Blood. The Church also asks that Christ's sacrifice be consumed for the salvation of those who partake of it.

- The *institution narrative and Consecration:* By repeating Christ's words and actions at the Last Supper, the sacrifice he instituted is perpetuated.

- The *anamnesis:* The Church fulfills Christ's memorial command by recalling his Passion, glorious Resurrection, and Ascension into heaven.

- The *oblation:* The Church offers the sinless eucharistic sacrifice through the Holy Spirit to the Father. The Church also intends that the faithful offer themselves so that, through the mediation of Christ, they can be brought into unity with God and with one another.

- The *intercessions:* The Eucharist is celebrated in communion with the whole Church, of both heaven and earth. All her members, living and dead, are called to participate in the redemption and salvation purchased by the body and blood of Christ.

- The *concluding doxology:* The glorification of God is expressed and is affirmed by the people's acclamation "Amen."

In his encyclical *Ecclesia de Eucharistia*, Pope St. John Paul II taught that "it is the ordained priest who, acting in the person of Christ, brings about the eucharistic sacrifice and offers it to God in the name of all the people. For this reason, the Roman Missal prescribes that only the priest should recite the Eucharistic Prayer, while the people participate in faith and in silence."[51]

According to the GIRM, "The nature of the presidential texts demands that they be spoken in a loud and clear voice and that everyone present listen with attention. While the priest is speaking these texts, there should be no other prayer or liturgical song, and the organ or other instruments should not be played."[52]

Many people ask exactly when during this part of Mass the bread and wine become the body and blood of Christ. According to the *Catechism*, this occurs as the priest utters the words of institution, or the words Jesus spoke at the Last Supper that include the phrase "this is my body." These words "[by] the power of the words and the action of Christ, and the power of the Holy Spirit, make sacramentally present under the species of bread and wine Christ's body and blood, his sacrifice offered on the cross once for all" (CCC 1353).

12. Under what circumstances can Catholics receive the Eucharist?

According to the Code of Canon Law, "Any baptized person not prohibited by law can and must be admitted to Holy Communion. The administration of the Most Holy Eucharist to children requires that they have sufficient knowledge and careful preparation so that they understand the mystery of Christ according to their capacity and are able to receive the body of Christ with faith and devotion. . . . A person who is conscious of grave sin is not to celebrate Mass or receive the body of the Lord without previous sacramental confession."[53]

Why does the Church prohibit receiving the Eucharist while in a state of mortal sin? St. Paul issued a stern warning to any who might receive the Eucharist in an unworthy or sinful way. He wrote, "Whoever, therefore, eats the bread or drinks the cup of the Lord in an unworthy manner will be guilty of profaning the body and blood of the Lord. Let a man examine himself, and so eat of the bread and drink of the cup. For any one who eats and drinks without discerning the body eats and drinks judgment upon himself. That is why many of you are weak and ill, and some have died" (1 Cor. 11:27–30).

Although the Eucharist does have the power to wipe away venial sin and minor imperfections in the soul, the Church teaches that anyone who is conscious of mortal sin (i.e., sin that is grave, freely chosen, and separates one from God's grace) should not receive the Eucharist.[54] While in a state of mortal sin, the person brings judgment upon himself when he consumes the very Savior he has forsaken through his sins. The *Code of Canon Law* says this person may not "receive the body of the Lord without prior sacramental confession unless a grave reason is present and there is no opportunity of confessing; in this case the person is to be mindful of the obligation to make an act of perfect contrition, including the intention of confessing as soon as possible."[55]

The obligation to attend Mass on Sundays and Holy Days is distinct from the obligation to receive the Eucharist. The Church requires a person to receive the Eucharist only once a year, usually during the Easter season. No one is obligated to receive the Eucharist at any particular Mass, because a person may be in a state of mortal sin or otherwise unprepared to receive. However, even if a person cannot receive the Eucharist physically, he can still make an act of spiritual communion and pray to receive Jesus into his heart. St. Teresa of Avila said, "When you do not receive Communion and you do not attend Mass, you can make a spiritual communion, which is a most beneficial practice; by it the love of God will be greatly impressed on you."[56]

It is also not required that a person attend Mass in order to receive the Eucharist. There are many reasons why people may be physically unable to attend Mass, and it would be unjust to deny them the grace of the sacrament just because of their inability to attend the liturgy. Sick or homebound people, for example, may have the Eucharist brought to them by a priest, deacon, acolyte, or other qualified person.

However, even if a person is not in the proper state to receive the Eucharist, he or she is still obligated to attend Mass. The Church "requires the faithful to sanctify the day commemorating the Resurrection of the Lord as well as the principal liturgical feasts honoring the mysteries of the Lord, the Blessed Virgin Mary, and the saints; in the first place, by participating in the Eucharistic celebration" (CCC 2042).

13. How should we receive the Eucharist?

Along with being properly disposed to receive the Eucharist by being free from the conscious knowledge of mortal sin, the faithful are required to fast before receiving the Eucharist. According to the *Code of Canon Law*, "A person who is to receive the Most Holy Eucharist is to abstain for at least one hour before holy communion from any food and drink, except for only water and medicine."[57] But the canon also specifically states that "the infirm" are not bound to observe the eucharistic fast.

Keep in mind that this is not a matter of revealed doctrine, but rather a discipline of the Church that can be changed. For most of Church history, the faithful fasted from midnight until they received the Eucharist the next morning. Only after that would they have a meal that would "break the fast" (i.e., breakfast). However, in 1953 Pope Pius XII reduced the period of fasting to three hours before Communion to encourage greater reception of the sacrament.[58] In 1964, Pope Paul VI changed the period of fasting once again, this time to one hour before Communion. The current *Code of Canon Law* says, "A person who is to receive the Most Holy Eucharist is to abstain for at least one hour before holy communion from any food and drink, except for only water and medicine."[59]

In regard to fasting *after* receiving the Eucharist, there is no specific rule on the matter, but a pious custom has arisen of not eating again until fifteen minutes after receiving Communion. This is done to allow the precious body and blood to dissolve in the stomach and cease to exist under the form of bread and wine (and thus cease to be the body and blood of Christ). A person who remains in church until Mass has concluded will usually fulfill this custom without even realizing it.

The GIRM states that when we go up to received the body and blood of the Lord: "the priest raises the host slightly and shows it to each, saying, *Corpus Christi* (the body of Christ). The communicant replies *Amen* and receives the sacrament either on the tongue or, where this is allowed and if the communicant so chooses, in the hand."[60]

This is a sacred act, and no priest or communicant can change the words uttered based on his personal preference. For example, a priest may not licitly raise the host and say, "Jesus Christ" or "Our Savior," but must instead say, "The body of Christ" (or a translation of the phrase in another language). Likewise, the communicant must say, "Amen" and not "Thanks" or "Peace be with you."[61]

The communicant traditionally received the body of the Lord on the tongue, but according to the GIRM, "the consecrated host may be received either on the tongue or in the hand, at the discretion of each communicant."[62] The only time reception in the hand is impermissible is in the case of intinction, that is, when the host is dipped in the precious blood and then placed on the communicant's tongue. Also, although reception in the hand is allowed, it is the universal law of the Latin rite that Communion is to be received on the tongue (unless an indult has been granted, as is the case in the United States, to allow reception in the hand), and no one, not even a priest, can forbid such reception.

In order to allow the Eucharist to be expediently dispensed, qualified laypersons may be allowed to distribute the body and blood of Christ. These people are not, however, called "eucharistic ministers," as only the priest is the minister of the Eucharist. The Congregation for the Divine Worship taught in *Redemptionis Sacramentum* that "this function is to be understood strictly according to the name by which it is known, that is to say, that of extraordinary minister of Holy Communion."[63]

14. How should unconsumed eucharistic elements be disposed of? What should be done if the body or blood of the Lord is spilled or coughed up?

Just as we should never take the Lord's name in vain, we should never treat the Lord himself in vain by acting in an irreverent or blasphemous way toward him when he is present with us in the sacrament of the Eucharist. That is why special care must be taken with the remaining elements of the precious body and precious blood after Mass has concluded.

The *Code of Canon Law* states: "A person who throws away the consecrated species or takes or retains them for a sacrilegious purpose incurs a *latae sententiae* [automatic] excommunication reserved to the Apostolic See; moreover, a cleric can be punished with another penalty, not excluding dismissal from the clerical state."[64] Keep in mind, however, that if a person did not know this was wrong, he would not be held accountable for his actions, and so he would not be automatically excommunicated.

In order to fully understand this law we must define what it means to "throw away" the consecrated bread and wine. Most people (but unfortunately not all people) understand that the body and blood of Christ should not be discarded in a trash bin or washed down a drain into the sewer. This would be a grave act of disrespect toward the body and blood of Christ. But many people mistakenly think that there are other licit ways to discard the consecrated species.

For example, some people believe that it is acceptable to bury the Eucharist in the ground or wash the precious blood down a sacrarium, a special sink in a church that does not lead to the sewer but drains into the earth. *Redemptionis Sacramentum* explicitly says that anyone "casting the sacred species into the sacrarium or in an unworthy place or on the ground, incurs the penalties laid down [in the Church's guidelines for excommunication]."[65]

So what should be done with leftover consecrated species? *Redemptionis Sacramentum* goes on to say, "whatever may remain of the Blood of Christ must be entirely and immediately consumed by the priest or by another minister, according to the norms, while the consecrated hosts that are left are to be consumed by the priest at the altar or carried to the place for the reservation of the Eucharist [i.e., the tabernacle]."

In the event that someone spills the precious blood, perhaps while serving Mass, the GIRM says, "The area should be washed and the water poured into the sacrarium."[66] This does not contradict the previous instruction not to pour the precious blood down the sacrarium, because once it is sufficiently mixed with water, the form of wine ceases to be and with it the precious blood present under that form also ceases to be. The elements that once constituted the precious blood may be poured down the sacrarium, just as other elements found in chalices and other liturgical wares are washed there.

The same rule applies to using water to wash a place where a partially digested or chewed eucharistic host has been expelled. The remnants of the host must be collected and then dissolved in water in the sacrarium. Even if this took place far from the sacrarium, it must still be done, because the body of Christ deserves nothing less.

Interestingly, if an insect such as a fly were to fall into the chalice, the priest has options other than to consume the creature. St. Thomas Aquinas said, "It ought to be poured out, and after purifying the chalice, fresh wine should be served for consecration. But if anything of the sort [should] happen after the consecration, the insect should be caught carefully and washed thoroughly, then burned, and the 'ablution,' together with the ashes, thrown into the sacrarium."[67]

15. Can non-Catholics receive the Eucharist?

A person must normally be baptized or received into

the Catholic Faith in order to receive the Eucharist and even then that person must be free from mortal sin or canonical penalties such as excommunication. For example, the *Didache* admonished first-century Christians to "let no one eat or drink of your Eucharist, unless they have been baptized into the name of the Lord; for concerning this also the Lord has said, 'Give not that which is holy to the dogs.'"[68]

Keep in mind that this rule is not carried out because of a sense of spiritual superiority or because the Church wants non-Catholics to feel bad. Instead, it is done out of a sense of concern for non-Catholics who might want to approach the sacrament.

The Catholic Church teaches that the Eucharist truly is the body and blood of Christ. When the communicant says "amen" upon receiving the Eucharist, he is saying that he believes not only in this tenet of the Faith, but also in all that the Catholic Church teaches. If he does not believe these things, then his consent to receiving the sacrament cannot be valid. Of course, if he desires the Eucharist, then he can always be received into the Catholic Church so that his communion with the Church will be as complete as his communion with Christ in the Eucharist.

A non-Catholic may receive the Eucharist only if he or she is a member of a church that holds the same view of the Eucharist as the Catholic Church. This is the case, for example, with Eastern Orthodox churches, whose bishops and priests retain valid apostolic authority but are in schism since they do not recognize the primacy and infallibility of Peter's successor in the bishop of Rome, the pope. It is licit to administer the sacraments of penance, anointing of the sick, and Eucharist to members of these churches, "if they seek such on their own accord and are properly disposed. This is also valid for members of other Churches which in the judgment of the Apostolic See are in the same condition in regard to the sacraments as these Eastern Churches."[69]

This may also be done for other Christians, such as a Protestant who wishes to convert to the Catholic faith (and thus believes in the Real Presence) but is in danger of dying. The *Code of Canon Law* states, "If the danger of death is present or if, in the judgment of the diocesan bishop or conference of bishops, some other grave necessity urges it, Catholic ministers administer these same sacraments [penance, Eucharist, and anointing of the sick] licitly also to other Christians not having full communion with the Catholic Church, who cannot approach a minister of their own community and who seek such on their own accord, provided that they manifest Catholic faith in respect to these sacraments and are properly disposed."[70]

The Church also teaches that under limited circumstances Catholics can receive the Eucharist in non-Catholic churches that have valid sacraments (e.g., Eastern Orthodox or Assyrian Church of the East, for example). This may be the case if someone is in a foreign country that lacks a Catholic presence and so is unable to attend Mass. The *Code of Canon Law* states that "whenever necessity requires or a genuine spiritual advantage commends it, and provided the danger of error or indifferentism is avoided, Christ's faithful for whom it is physically or morally impossible to approach a Catholic minister, may lawfully receive the sacraments of penance, the Eucharist, and anointing of the sick from non-Catholic ministers in whose Churches these sacraments are valid."[71]

16. What kind of bread and wine can be used at Mass?

Christ desires all people to be able to receive his grace through the sacraments of the Church. But a problem arises when people have physical impediments that prevent them from receiving the sacraments, including the Eucharist. For example, those with celiac disease risk severe intestinal damage if they ingest gluten, which is the protein in wheat (as well as barley and rye) that makes processed grains doughy. Likewise, alcoholics who consume even a small amount of wine risk "falling off the wagon" and engaging in their previous alcoholic behaviors. So should the Church offer "gluten-free" Communion wafers and nonalcoholic wine?

According to the *Code of Canon Law*, "The most holy Eucharistic sacrifice must be offered with bread and with wine in which a little water must be mixed. The bread must be only wheat and recently made so that there is no danger of spoiling. The wine must be natural from the fruit of the vine and not spoiled."[72] The GIRM further elaborates on what is required of the wine that is used at Mass. It says, "The wine for the Eucharistic celebration must be from the fruit of the grapevine (cf. Luke 22:18), natural, and unadulterated—that is, without admixture of extraneous substances."[73] This often means that the wine should be purchased from vendors who have experience with wine used in the liturgy, since ordinary commercial wine may contain foreign substances that spoil it for the Eucharist.

So what can be done for the people who suffer from celiac disease or for communicants or priests who struggle with alcoholism? In 1994, the Congregation for the Doctrine of the Faith released a document called *Norms for Use of Low-Gluten Bread and Mustum*. The document says, "Low-gluten hosts are valid matter, provided that they contain the amount of gluten sufficient to obtain the confection of bread, that there is no addition of foreign materials and that the procedure for making such hosts is not such as to alter the nature of the substance of the bread." Regarding wine, the norms say that a priest, when given permission by the bishop, may use mustum in place of normal wine. Mustum is a "fresh juice from grapes or juice preserved by suspending its fermentation (by means of freezing or other methods which do not alter its nature)." It is not "grape juice" but wine whose fermentation has been suspended, thus drastically reducing its alcohol content.

In addition, people who are both allergic to wheat and unable to receive alcohol can always make an act of *spiritual communion*. St. Thomas Aquinas advocated for the practice, and the Council of Trent approved it.[74] But people who are unable to receive only one of the consecrated species can receive the Eucharist under either the form of bread or the form of wine. This is possible because the consecrated bread and the consecrated wine each fully become Christ's entire person: body, blood, soul, and divinity. According to the United States Conference of Catholic Bishops:

> It should never be construed, therefore, that Communion under the form of bread alone or Communion under the form of wine alone is somehow an incomplete act or that Christ is not fully present to the communicant. The Church's unchanging teaching from the time of the Fathers through the ages . . . has witnessed to a constant unity of faith in the presence of Christ in both elements.[75]

Lastly, in 1439 the Ecumenical Council of Florence declared that "the body of Christ is truly confected in both unleavened and leavened wheat bread, and priests should confect the body of Christ in either, that is, each priest according to the custom of his Western or Eastern church."[76] In the West, it is customary to use flat, unleavened bread because that is what Jesus used (and Jews still use today) at Passover. In the East, it is customary to use fluffy, leavened bread because it symbolizes the life of the spirit that is raised through the Eucharist. Both are valid disciplines in their respective rites within the Catholic Church.

17. What did the Second Vatican Council teach about the Eucharist?

The Mass and the sacrament of the Eucharist are discussed throughout the documents of the Second Vatican Council. For example, the Constitution on the Sacred Liturgy, *Sacrosanctum Concilium*, teaches that the Eucharist holds a central place in the life of the Church. It says:

> The liturgy is the summit toward which the activity of the Church is directed; at the same time it is the font from which all her power flows. For the aim and object of apostolic works is that all who are made sons of God by faith and baptism should come together to praise God in the midst of his Church, to take part in the sacrifice, and to eat the Lord's supper.[77]

The Decree on the Ministry and Life of Priests, or

Presbyterorum Ordinis, also testifies to the uniqueness and centrality of this sacrament. It says:

> The other sacraments, as well as with every ministry of the Church and every work of the apostolate, are tied together with the Eucharist and are directed toward it. The Most Blessed Eucharist contains the entire spiritual boon of the Church, that is, Christ himself, our Pasch and Living Bread, by the action of the Holy Spirit through his very flesh vital and vitalizing, giving life to men who are thus invited and encouraged to offer themselves, their labors and all created things, together with him.[78]

If the Eucharist holds such a central place in the life of the Church, and the Eucharist can exist only when bread and wine are consecrated by a priest with valid holy orders, then it logically follows that the mission of the priest is also central to the life of the Church. *Ad Gentes*, the Decree on the Missionary Activity of the Church, puts it this way: "By means of their own ministry—which consists principally in the Eucharist which perfects the Church—they are in communion with Christ the Head and are leading others to this communion."[79]

One mistaken idea that arose after the council was that Christ is equally present in the Word or even in the people at Mass and in the Eucharist, thus, just as we don't genuflect before our fellow brothers and sisters at Mass, there is no need to genuflect before the tabernacle that contains the Eucharist. This erroneous belief may be one of the reasons Pope Paul VI issued the encyclical *Mysterium Fidei* during the council. It rebukes this teaching in the following passage:

> These various ways in which Christ is present fill the mind with astonishment and offer the Church a mystery for her contemplation. But there is another way in which Christ is present in his Church, a way that surpasses all the others. It is his presence in the Sacrament of the Eucharist, which is, for this reason, "a more consoling source of devotion, a lovelier object of contemplation and holier in what it contains" than all the other sacraments; for it contains Christ himself and it is "a kind of consummation of the spiritual life, and in a sense the goal of all the sacraments." This presence is called "real" not to exclude the idea that the others are "real" too, but rather to indicate presence par excellence, because it is substantial and through it Christ becomes present whole and entire, God and man.[80]

18. What is eucharistic adoration?

The Church, of course, adores the Eucharist at every Mass, and treats it with adoring reverence whenever it is transported. The practice popularly called "eucharistic adoration" refers specifically to praying before the Eucharist outside of a liturgical setting, when it has been reserved or exposed in a sacred vessel.

The first recorded instance of eucharistic adoration took place on September 11, 1226, when, "in compliance with the wish of Louis VII, who had just been victorious over the Albigensians [a group of heretics], the Blessed Sacrament, veiled, was exposed in the Chapel of the Holy Cross, as an act of thanksgiving. So great was the throng of adorers that the bishop, Pierre de Corbie, judged it expedient to continue the adoration by night, as well as by day, a proposal that was subsequently ratified by the approval of the Holy See."[81]

Eucharistic adoration can take place with the Blessed Sacrament exposed in a gold container called a monstrance, or unexposed and kept in the tabernacle. The word *tabernacle* means "dwelling place"; there is even a feast of tabernacles in Judaism, that is also called the feast of booths or, in Hebrew, *Sukkot*. During one part of this feast, temporary shelters are erected in honor of the tents the Israelites dwelled in as they sojourned through the desert. It's fitting, then, that the Eucharist is given its own "dwelling place" in the form of the tabernacle.

According to the *Code of Canon Law*, "The tabernacle in which the Most Holy Eucharist is reserved is to be situated in some part of the church or oratory which is distinguished, conspicuous, beautifully decorated, and suitable for prayer." It should also be "immovable, made of solid or opaque material, and locked so that the danger of profanation may be entirely avoided."[82]

The *Code of Canon Law* also says, "A special lamp which indicates and honors the presence of Christ is to shine continuously before a tabernacle in which the Most Holy Eucharist is reserved."[83] According to the GIRM, this lamp should be "fueled by oil or wax, [and] should be kept alight to indicate and honor the presence of Christ."[84] This means that the lamp should generally not be an electric light or candle, though such devices are not explicitly forbidden. The lamp has traditionally been red, but there is no liturgical law or precept that requires it to be any particular color.

During the period of adoration, the faithful may offer up either spontaneous prayers or formal prayers such as the rosary. However, the Eucharist may not be exposed for the sole purpose of formal prayers. The Congregation for Divine Worship in the 1998 edition of *Notitiae* said, "One should not expose the Eucharist only to recite the rosary. However, among the prayers that are used during adoration, the recitation of the rosary may certainly be included, emphasizing the Christological aspects with biblical readings relating to the mysteries, and providing time for silent adoration and meditation on them."

When the Eucharist is exposed for longer periods of time, it is called perpetual adoration. But this should be done only when there is a reasonable certainty that someone will always be able to worship in the presence of the sacrament and not leave it unattended. *Redemptionis Sacramentum* says that "the Most Holy Sacrament, when exposed, must never be left unattended even for the briefest space of time. It should therefore be arranged that at least some of the faithful always be present at fixed times, even if they take alternating turns."[85]

19. Have there been miracles involving the Eucharist?

Although there have been no miracles involving the Eucharist that the Church has required Catholics to believe as articles of faith, there have been several reports of miracles that the Church has investigated and deemed appropriate for Catholics to accept. Here are just a few of them:[86]

- *Lanciano, Italy, 8th century:* During Mass, the consecrated bread and wine became actual flesh and blood. The host and globules of blood were preserved and are on display to this very day. A team of researchers in the 1970s and '80s examined the host and determined that the flesh came from a human heart and the blood was type AB.

- *Bolsena-Orvieta, Italy, 1263:* A German priest named Peter of Prague was struggling with the doctrine of transubstantiation when suddenly, while he was saying Mass, blood slowly began to emerge from the host at the moment of Consecration. Pope Urban IV called for an investigation into the matter and declared it to be authentic. He later commissioned St. Thomas Aquinas to compose both the Office for the Mass and the Liturgy of the Hours for a feast called Corpus Christi, which would be dedicated to the Eucharist. Even today, during the feast of Corpus Christi the cathedral in Orvieto exposes the linen stained with the blood from the host held by Peter of Prague.

- *Avignon, France, 1433:* After several days of heavy rain, the entire city of Avignon was flooded—except for a path leading into the church where the Eucharist was being kept for perpetual adoration. The religious brothers who run the small church still celebrate this miracle by exposing the sacrament and singing a chant from the Canticle of Moses, which was originally sung when God miraculously kept the waters of the Red Sea at bay during the Exodus.

- *Eten, Peru, 1649:* Fr. Jerome Silva saw an image of a child on the eucharistic host, and an apparition of the divine child Jesus was also reported to have appeared to several people. This miracle is celebrated in Eten every year on July 12.

- *Trivandrum, India, 2001:* Fr. Johnson Karoor saw

three dots and later a human face on the Eucharist while he was saying Mass. In an interview, Fr. Karoor said, "I didn't have the strength to speak anything to the faithful. I stood aside for some time. I couldn't control my tears. We had the practice of reading Scripture and reflecting on it during adoration. The passage that I got that day as I opened the Bible was John 20:24–29, Jesus appearing to St. Thomas and asking him to see his wounds."

Finally, it is important to remember that at every Mass a miracle occurs even if we can't perceive it. That's because after Consecration the substance of the bread and wine ceases to exist and is replaced with the substance of Christ's body and blood.

20. How can I develop a greater devotion to the Eucharist?

The easiest way to develop a greater devotion to the Eucharist is to attend daily Mass, so you can partake of Christ's body and blood on a regular basis. You can also take part in a holy hour at a local chapel that hosts perpetual adoration or the Forty Hours Devotion."This devotion takes place, as its name suggests, for forty hours after the sacrament is exposed. In Scripture, the number forty symbolizes the transformation of holy people, such as when the Israelites wandered for forty years in the desert or when Jesus fasted in the desert for forty days. Likewise, through the Forty Hours Devotion, the worshipper can take part in a spiritual transformation by spending time adoring the Lord (though he is not obligated remain in adoration for the entire forty hours).

You can also read theological and ecclesial writings about the Eucharist—works by theologians such as Louis Bouyer (his book on the subject is called *Eucharist: Theology and Spirituality of the Eucharistic Prayer*) or papal documents such as Pope St. John Paul II's encyclical *Ecclesia de Eucharistia*. Finally, when you attend Mass you can offer up the following prayer, which has been attributed to Padre Pio after he received Christ in the Eucharist:

Stay with me, Lord, for it is necessary to have you present so that I do not forget you. You know how easily I abandon you.

Stay with me, Lord, because I am weak, and I need your strength, so that I may not fall so often.

Stay with me, Lord, for you are my life, and without you, I am without fervor.

Stay with me, Lord, for you are my light, and without you, I am in darkness.

Stay with me, Lord, to show me your will.

Stay with me, Lord, so that I may hear your voice and follow you.

Stay with me, Lord, for I desire to love you very much and always be in your company.

Stay with me, Lord, if you wish me to be faithful to you.

Stay with me, Lord, for as poor as my soul is, I want it to be a place of consolation for you, a nest of love.

Stay with me, Jesus, for it is getting late, and the day is coming to a close, and life passes, death, judgment, eternity approach. It is necessary to renew my strength, so that I will not stop along the way, and for that, I need you. It is getting late and death approaches. I fear the darkness, the temptations, the dryness, the cross, the sorrows. Oh, how I need you, my Jesus, in this night of exile.

Stay with me tonight, Jesus; in life with all its dangers, I need you.

Let me recognize you as your disciples did at the breaking of bread, so that the eucharistic communion may be the light which disperses the darkness, the force which sustains me, the unique joy of my heart.

Stay with me, Lord, because at the hour of my death, I want to remain united to you, if not by communion, at least by grace and love.

Stay with me, Jesus, I do not ask for divine consolation because I do not merit it, but the gift of your presence, oh yes, I ask this of you.

Stay with me, Lord, for it is you alone I look for, your love, your grace, your will, your heart, your spirit, because I love you and ask no other reward but to love you more and more.

With a firm love, I will love you with all my heart while on earth and continue to love you perfectly during all eternity. Amen.

About the Author

Trent Horn is an apologist and speaker for Catholic Answers. He specializes in pro-life issues as well as outreach to atheists and agnostics. He holds a master's degree in theology from Franciscan University of Steubenville.

Endnotes

1 Bart Brewer, "The Mystery of the Eucharist," mtc.org/eucharst.html.

2 William Lane Craig vs. Sam Harris, "Is the Foundation of Morality Natural or Supernatural?," debate at University of Notre Dame, Notre Dame, Indiana, April 2011, http://www.reasonablefaith.org/is-the-foundation-of-morality-natural-or-supernatural-the-craig-harris#ixzz3iQGTiOw5.

3 Center for Applied Research in the Apostolate (CARA), Georgetown University, "Sacraments Today: Belief and Practice Among U.S. Catholics," http://cara.georgetown.edu/sacraments.html.

4 The Salvation Army cannot be considered a Christian denomination because it does not teach that its members should be baptized. The New Testament makes it clear that baptism is what brings us into God's family and takes away original sin (1 Pet. 3:21; John 3:5; Rom. 6; and so on). Even Protestant denominations that deny baptismal regeneration usually still baptize because Jesus commanded that this be done (Matt. 28:19).

5 John Dart, "Salvation Army OKs Freedom to Practice Popular Sacraments," *Los Angeles Times*, May 30, 1998, http://articles.latimes.com/1998/may/30/local/me-54789.

6 Russell D. Moore, "Christ's Presence as Memorial," *Understanding Four Views on the Lord's Supper*, ed. John H. Armstrong (Grand Rapids, Mich.: Zondervan, 2007), 38.

7 *Westminster Confession of Faith* 29:7.

8 Martin Luther, "Confession Concerning Christ's Supper" in *Word and Sacrament* III, ed. Robert H. Fischer, vol. 37 of *Luther's Works*, ed. Jaroslav Pelikan and Helmut T. Lehmann (Philadel-

phia: Fortress Press, 1961), 299–300.

9   Council of Trent, Session XIII, Chapter 4.

10 Although at times an appeal to mystery is made and terms are
    avoided, sometimes the word *metousiosis*, meaning a change of
    essence, is used, and sometimes the word *transubstantiation*, but
    it is qualified. For example, the nineteenth-century St. Philaret's
    Catechism says, "The word transubstantiation is not to be taken to
    define the manner in which the bread and wine are changed into
    the Body and Blood of the Lord; for this none can understand but
    God; but only thus much is signified, that the bread truly, really,
    and substantially becomes the very true Body of the Lord, and the
    wine the very Blood of the Lord."

11 Martin Luther, "The Babylonian Captivity of the Church," *Works
    of Martin Luther,* Vol. 2, eds. Henry Ester Jacobs and Adolph
    Spaeth (Philadelphia: A.J. Holman, 1915), 190.

12 Fourth Lateran Council, *Confession of Faith.*

13 Council of Trent, Session XIII, Chapter 4.

14 Origen, *Against Celsus* 6:27.

15 St. Justin Martyr, *First Apology* 26.

16 Available online at http://www.merriam-webster.com/dictionary/
    cannibalism.

17 Stephen K. Ray, *Crossing the Tiber: Evangelical Protestants Dis-
    cover the Historical Church* (San Francisco: Ignatius Press, 1997),
    210.

18 Brant Pitre, *Jesus and the Jewish Roots of the Eucharist* (New York:
    Doubleday, 2011), 144–145.

19 Giles Dimock, *101 Questions & Answers on the Eucharist* (New
    York: Paulist Press, 2006), 52.

20 *Summa Theologica* III:81:1.

21 The original Greek word is *epiousios*, which is found for the first time in this passage, and so its original meaning is not well known. Jerome and Cyril of Alexandria rendered it "supersubstantial," because etymologically *epiousios* means "above" (*epi*) "substance or nature" (*ousia*). See also Pitre, *Jesus and the Jewish Roots of the Eucharist*, 92–96.

22 This argument is found in Eric Svendsen, *Evangelical Answers: A Critique of Current Roman Catholic Apologists* (Lindenhurst: Reformation Press, 1999), 180.

23 Pitre, *Jesus and the Jewish Roots of the Eucharist*, 103–104. Another point Pitre covers is the issue of drinking Christ's blood. He writes, "I suggest that the very reason God forbids drinking blood in the Old Testament is the same reason Jesus commands his disciples to drink his blood: 'For the life [Hebrew *nephesh*] of the flesh is in the blood' (Leviticus 17:11). Jesus would have known the Law of Moses, and he would have known that the power of his own resurrected 'life'—indeed, his 'soul'—was in his blood. Therefore, *if the disciples wished to share in the 'life' of Jesus' bodily resurrection, then they had to partake of both his body and his blood*" (115).

24 Norman Geisler and Ralph MacKenzie, *Roman Catholics and Evangelicals: Agreements and Differences* (Grand Rapids, Mich.: Baker Books, 1995), 261–262.

25 Ibid., 262.

26 Karl Keating, *Catholicism and Fundamentalism: The Assault on "Romanism" by "Bible Christians"* (San Francisco: Ignatius Press, 1988), 242.

27 J.N.D. Kelly, *Early Christian Doctrines* (New York: HarperCollins, 1978), 440.

28 Darwell Stone, *The Holy Communion* (London: Longmans, Green, and Co., 1904), 37.

29 St. Ignatius of Antioch, *Letter to the Smyrnaeans* 7:1.

30 St. Justin Martyr, *First Apology* 66.

31 St. Irenaeus, *Against Heresies* 4:33:2.

32 Origen, *Homilies on Numbers* 7:2.

33 Bartholomew F. Brewer, Ph.D., *The Mystery of the Eucharist*, http://mtc.org/eucharst.html.

34 St. Ambrose, *On the Mysteries* 9:53.

35 William Webster, *The Church of Rome at the Bar of History* (Carlisle, Penn.: Banner of Truth, 1997), 119.

36 Tertullian, *Against Marcion*, Book IV, Chapter 40.

37 Kelly, *Early Christian Doctrines*, 442.

38 Webster, *The Church of Rome at the Bar of History*, 120.

39 Brewer, *The Mystery of the Eucharist*.

40 Jack Chick. *The Death Cookie*, https://www.chick.com/reading/tracts/0074/0074_01.asp.

41 In Greek, Jesus' name is Iesous. The first three letters are iota (*I*), eta (*H*), and sigma (*S*). In capital letters the Greek letter eta is represented with an *H*.

42 Justin Martyr, *First Apology* 66.

43 Manfred Clauss. *The Roman Cult of Mithras* (New York: Routledge, 2001), 109.

44 Ibid., 115. This is confirmed by the presence of animal bones at the site of these communion meals.

45 John R. Hinnells, "Reflections on the Bull-Slaying Scene,"

Mithraic Studies, vol. 2. For more information on these topics see Jon Sorensen's articles, "Horus Manure: Debunking the Jesus/Horus Connection," in the Nov/Dec 2012 issue of *Catholic Answers* Magazine, and "Exploding the Mithras Myth" in the May/June 2013 issue.

46 *Ecclesia de Eucharistia* 11.

47 *Didache* 14.

48 St. Cyprian of Carthage, *Letters* 63:14.

49 St. Augustine, *Letters* 98:9.

50 "The Liturgy of the Eucharist," http://www.usccb.org/prayer-and-worship/the-mass/order-of-mass/liturgy-of-the-eucharist/.

51 *Ecclesia de Eucharistia* 28.

52 *General Instruction of the Roman Missal* (GIRM) 32.

53 *Code of Canon Law* (CIC) 912–913, 916.

54 "As bodily nourishment restores lost strength, so the Eucharist strengthens our charity, which tends to be weakened in daily life; and this living charity wipes away venial sins" (CCC 1394).

55 CIC 916. The *Code of Canon Law* also says that "those who are excommunicated or interdicted after the imposition or declaration of the penalty and others who obstinately persist in manifest grave sin are not to be admitted to Holy Communion" (CIC 915).

56 St. Teresa of Avila, *The Way of Perfection* 35:1. Cited in *Ecclesia de Eucharistia* 34.

57 CIC 919.

58 *Christus Dominus, Concerning the Discipline to Be Observed with Respect to the Eucharistic Fast*, 13. This was later extended in the 1957 motu propio *Sacram Communionem*.

59 CIC 919.

60 GIRM 160–161.

61 Ibid., 117.

62 Ibid., 160.

63 *Redemptionis Sacramentum* 156.

64 CIC 1382.

65 *Redemptionis Sacramentum* 107.

66 GIRM 280.

67 *Summa Theologica* III:83:6. Thomas also says in this section that
     if the precious blood is determined to have been poisoned, "the
     priest should neither receive it nor administer it to others on any
     account, lest the life-giving chalice become one of death, but it
     ought to be kept in a suitable vessel with the relics: and in order
     that the sacrament may not remain incomplete, he ought to put
     other wine into the chalice, resume the Mass from the consecra-
     tion of the blood, and complete the sacrifice."

68 *Didache* 9.

69 CIC 844.3.

70 CIC 844.4.

71 CIC 844.2.

72 CIC 924. Dimock explains, "Because the Lord became flesh in
     first-century Palestine, born into a Jewish family, that history,
     that symbolism, that rich tradition, still shapes our sacramental
     and liturgical life." *101 Questions & Answers on the Eucharist*, 18.

73 GIRM 322.

74 See *Summa Theologica* III:80:2 and Council of Trent, Session
     XIII, Chapter 8.

75 *Norms for the Distribution and Reception of Holy Communion
     Under Both Kinds in the Dioceses of the United States of America*, 15.

76 Council of Florence, Session VI.

77 *Sacrosanctum Conciliam* 10.

78 *Presbyterorum Ordinis* 5.

79 *Ad Gentes* 39.

80 *Mysterium Fidei* 38–39.

81 Joseph McMahon, "Perpetual Adoration," *Catholic Encyclopedia*, Vol. 1 (New York: Robert Appleton Company, 1907), http://www.newadvent.org/cathen/01152a.htm.

82 CIC 938.

83 CIC 940.

84 GIRM 316.

85 *Redemptionis Sacramentum* 138.

86 These accounts come from Ron Rychlak, "Eucharistic Miracles: Evidence of the Real Presence," *This Rock*, Vol. 17, no. 7, September 2006, and "Eucharistic Miracles," available online at http://www.therealpresence.org/eucharst/mir/a3.html.

What Is Catholic Answers?

Catholic Answers is a media ministry that serves Christ by explaining and defending the Catholic faith:

- We help Catholics grow in their faith
- We bring former Catholics home
- We lead non-Catholics into the fullness of the truth

There are many ways we help people:

 Catholic Answers Live is America's most popular Catholic radio program

 Catholic Answers Press publishes faith-building books, booklets, magazines, and audio resources

 Catholic Answers Studios creates television programs, DVDs, and online videos

 Our website, Catholic.com hosts hundreds of thousands of online resources, free to use

 Catholic Answers Events conducts seminars, conferences, and pilgrimages

Catholic Answers is an independent, nonprofit organization supported by your donations.

Visit us online and learn how we can help you.

Your journey starts at:
catholic.com

Become part of the team.
Help support Catholic Answers.

Catholic Answers is an apostolate dedicated to serving Christ by bringing the fullness of Catholic truth to the world. We help good Catholics become better Catholics, bring former Catholics "home," and lead non-Catholics into the fullness of the Faith.

Catholic Answers neither asks for nor receives financial support from any diocese. The majority of its annual income is in the form of donations from individual supporters like you.

To make a donation by phone using your credit card, please speak with one of our customer service representatives at 888-291-8000.

To make a donation by check, please send a check payable to "Catholic Answers" to:

Catholic Answers
2020 Gillespie Way
El Cajon, CA 92020

To make a donation online, visit **catholic.com**.

TO EXPLAIN & DEFEND THE FAITH

catholic.com

HELP GET PEOPLE BACK TO MASS!

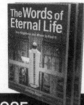

GREAT RESOURCE FOR THOSE SEEKING SOMETHING REAL & TRUE

This little booklet can show friends and family *True Happiness and Where to Find It*. Single copies are free at catholic.com. Buy multiple copies for $1 each.

Here's how to use it:

- Put copies in church literature racks and pews.
- Give copies to friends and relatives.
- Make a gift to your parish of a copy for each family!

In times of turmoil, when nothing seems normal or certain about our jobs, our health, our beliefs, or the future of our planet, true happiness—and the tranquil peace that comes with it—can seem even more elusive.

In *The Words of Eternal Life*, Jimmy Akin takes an unflinching look at the problem and offers a solution that is daring and radical, yet familiar and available anywhere, for free, right now. The answer is Jesus, the Word of the Father who teaches us the words of eternal life; the Word made flesh who by the words of a priest comes to dwell among us and feed us with the grace of peace and strength.

Written in a clear, inviting style that speaks equally to religiously unaffiliated inquirers and to believers who may have let their faith get lukewarm or go out of practice, *The Words of Eternal Life* is a great resource to give loved ones looking for something real and true—or to give your own faith life a helpful boost.

ORDER NOW IN BULK
$1 EACH (CASE OF 100)
OR $3.95 EACH

shop.catholic.com
To place an order, simply visit our safe and secure online shop

844.239.4952
Representatives can answer product questions & take your order by phone